If Death Could Sweep Me Off My Feet

MaryAnn Johnson

BookLeaf Publishing

Presentation by *BookLeaf Publishing*

Web: www.bookleafpub.com

E-mail: info@bookleafpub.com

ISBN: 9789357696449

First edition 2022

DEDICATION

To Grandpa Jr. for showing me how to see the beautiful art that life has to offer us. To answer your question Grandpa Jr. I want to be a writer when I grow up.

PREFACE

Written after a major death in my life at 14 then read
at my grandfathers funeral at 20:

If all the stars in the sky
Represent the souls taken from our side
I hope yours is the brightest one.
Because when we lay you down tonight
Tears will even fall from the sky.
And as we wipe them away
We will laugh and rejoice
Remembering the sound of your voice
That will never be forgotten.
It will take so long
To again hear your favorite song.
But don't you worry about me
For one day my sad will be replaced with the glee
That I even knew
An amazing person like you.
Even though you passed away
Your imprint is here to stay
Now your pain is gone
And the sunrise is all yours at dawn
Wherever your body lies
The universe will let you paint the skies
Until you're brought to your next life
And your soul is placed in the sky
Where You can look down on us from up so high

But let the stars
Heal our scars
And our broken hearts
By reminding us that your body is cold
And your voice is gone
But your soul lives on
In the brightest star in the sky
That represents your soul that was taken from our
side.

After the December Deaths

grief drenched me in gasoline.
every year when the chill
of december breathes in
and the numbing of the cold air settles
i strike the matches and light myself up
like the lights on a Christmas tree,
that mock me with their brightness and joy.
i let my soaked body burn and burn
keeping me warm,
lighting the shortened days,
allowing me to burn away,
peel off my own skin,
and break the cycle to start new
come springtime again.

Little New Red Shoes

down the long red carpet
of the dark church
there was a table.
a table with
many things,
 and photos,
and memories.

but one thing stuck out the most,

it was these little, new, red shoes.
far too red
to be amongst
 the crowd of people in all black.
far too new
to never be worn again,
and far, far too little
to belong to
ashes upon an urn.

My First School Friend

i
sitting here, tripping
over my own thoughts
my mind wanders in a daze.
there my hand was reaching out
to someone who was already lost.
we were once friends, now acquaintances,
well now she's the Dead Girl,
so, i'm not sure if any title still stands,
all i know is if i don't get help,
i'll never open my eyes,
i will always be falling after her with one arm
reached out trying to save the dead,
and the other arm desperately outstretched
to be saved by the living.

ii
stepped into my grave and fell face first into forever.
i sometimes still see her when i close my eyes.
she lives in me and reminds me, but i can't help but to
wonder,
what if i lived inside her mind? would she still be
alive?
i just hope that whatever she believed in was true.
that she reconnected with her mother,
lived a life after this dreadful one she was placed in.
bury me in the dirt, let my body rot,
for it never saved her neither did time

which they say heals all, but really, she never
gave time the time of day, she took matters to her
own hands
that day she jumped into the pond.

Like a Second Father

You left us so unexpectedly.
The days leading up to your funeral
were full with many claims such as,
"He was too young,"
"He was a good friend"
"He was a good husband."
"He was a good father,"
"He was a good man"
You were too young,
you were a good friend, husband, father, and man.
Weeks after the funeral and we found out
that you were a good liar too.
I had to hold this knowledge from your children,
my friends.
For weeks everyone who found out the truth,
fought to decide who to remember,
the only you we ever knew,
or the you who had a secret kid with a secret woman?
Do we believe and remember your truth, our truth,
Or the truth?

Tales of a Grieving Family

i.   Early Mourning
You always asked my siblings and I,
What do you want to be when you grow up?
Shrugging shoulders and you agreed with us,
We thought this was funny.
Now there is no more growing up for you
Only the growing of new
Tumors every day and a job you push yourself to
keep,
How can a man who's always had life and ambition
just be dying?
Did you ever figure out what you wanted to be
When you grew up?
I did Grandpa jr. I am going to be a teacher
But I want to be a writer
Your first granddaughter is having a child
Your first great grandchild is going to third grade,
I might finally graduate
Stick around to meet him,
Stick around watch them all reach middle school
Stick around for your grandkids to get through
college,
Stick around and I'll have a book for you to read.
Wrinkled hands and a scratchy voice never stopped
you before
But damn this chemo might,
You've grown up, but we haven't

We know what we want to be we think
I want to be a writer
Stick around to be a reader, please

Stick around and read this for me.

ii.	Silence of Grief
Hospital bands put on too tight,
A Ventilator down the throat.
Rows of pill bottles on the dresser,
The same Gold Jesus on a cross.
His voice sounds higher from the fear,
Her hair looks greyer from the grief
Everyone has stopped eating
Everyone's gone quiet

iii.	Bella
My grandfather's dog,
Whom my mother did not want on the bed
Jumped up and snuggled by her side
Just as if she were my grandfather
She was my grandfather
She was his work ethic,
Passion for art,
Dedication to people
She was his shadow in all the wonderful aways
But to this dog, she was a warm body to snuggle next
to,
While the baby lay loudly awake babbling in the next
room.

iv.   Room 10307
Blue lips,
Beeping oxygen machines,
Failing hearts and falling tears
A room full of admirers,
A room full of sorrow as we say
Goodbyes.

v.   11.20.21
How do we say goodbye?
Reminiscing memories the stories you told a
thousand times
How do we say goodbye?
Appreciate the sunrises and the clouds at night,
How do we just say goodbye?
He said he lived a good life he said he has no regrets
So let's leave ours behind
As we all take a deep breath
And say
"see you later,"

The Last Time I Prayed

the last time i prayed, i was
down on my shaking knees,
desperate tears escaping my squeezed shut eyes,
with my hands forced together so tightly,
that my knuckles were turning red;
as if that would somehow boost a signal, and
i cried "dear god, could you
make him feel no more pain.
it's not fair to him,"

the last time i prayed,
the little boys family
held a funeral days later,
with the minister up at the
front of the church,
preaching to the grieving faces;
"he is no longer in pain."
"this boy is in a better place now,"
"god has stopped his pain,"

that's not what i meant.

with a bowed head, wide open eyes,
and unclenched hands, i hear as the echoes
of every soft, sad voice begin to pray--
every voice but mine.

Grieving People Need to Eat too

silver tin pans line the cluttered counters of
the newly widow's chaotic and full,
yet, now lonely home.
my mother stands tiredly at the end of the table
filled with bottomless pans of food
and sad smiling children.
she's the stand in mom for a mourning friend,
lecturing about how "grieving people need to eat
too."
she scoops plates full of steamed carrots, honey
glazed ham,
chicken stuffing, creamy mashed potatoes,
over cooked turkey and various other holiday foods.
scraping forks and sweet chatter fill the room.
old memories of eldon swirl around like
that time when he learned all the words to a
macklemore song, and
the way the kids would run and hug him after a long
shift at the railroad.
these stories fluttered from the same mouths that
feast on meals provided by families who were still
whole.
circumstances as bitter as the cranberry sauce from
the jones's
memories as sweet as the pumpkin pie from the
hilman's.
for the first time in three days,
everyone is smiling and
every plate across the table sits crumb free.

Soft Dark Grey

When the little blue line went flat
I waited for your gasp of air,
My aunt prayed for a miracle,
We all prayed for the end of suffering,
I never really prayed but I hoped and
I remember thinking that maybe
Had I died when I was supposed to
That they would all still be here and
I remember being suffocated alive
But the overwhelming feeling
Of wanting not quite to die
But not live, but that wouldn't bring you back
Nothing would, nothing could
And honestly, it's not fair,
Christmas first now thanksgiving
They are gone they are ruined
They are tainted they are painted
In the colors of grief, a soft, dark, grey
The color of regret turning to forgiveness,
The idea of denial, bargaining, depression, anger
Turning into a beautiful shade of dark yellow
Filling shovels full of people ready to go
And people taken too early all turning
Into a sunset painted color of acceptance.

Take Me Away

If death could sweep me off my feet
Without ever inflicting pain onto you
I'd never touch the ground again.

Greatness

13

All in all,
Death really only brings great things.
Great sadness,
Great parties,
Great pain,
Great forgiveness,
Great food,
And great poetry.

The Drive Home

I remember everything that day. I remember my mother's casserole, the Facebook post, the music, the Christmas music, the smell of cigarette smoke, hospital smell, the dim room, the dazed switch in her eyes, the punch to the wall, the pacing, the movie we watched, the tears, the honest truth, the cold dead truth, the reality of it all, I remember the feelings of every person there entering into my 14 year old body and causing everything to shut down because I don't remember the drive home.

Thirty Minutes

15

Emily Dickinson said that we all get an hour.
There has been many times in my life
Where I was not so sure I deserved an hour.
Although, something I am very certain of,
Is that you deserved much more,
Than the thirty minutes you got.

I Miss the Kitchen Talks

16

Thanksgiving's here
I've spent many without him
But now he's gone
And it feels so lonely
in the kitchen
it's so hard
to even imagine
an empty life
and an empty kitchen

How to be Happy

i will not lie to you, it really bothers me
that i have to take a little orange pill to be happy.

it bothers me that i'm not sure if it's working,
because i cannot remember simple happiness
only emptiness, with bursts of joy.

i'm so sorry mom and dad, you gave me a good life
my brain is broken. i just hope you know i really
tried.

i tried to be better. i tried to be happy. a doctor and
some friends told me they were worried so now i
have to take a little orange pill to keep me here on
this earth.

it just bothers me
that i never learned how to be happy.

Let My Brain Wander

What if my mom dies?
Have you ever repeated that
To yourself a thousand times?
Over and over again
When you lay in bed at night?
What if my mom dies,
What if my best friend dies?
What if my dad, brother, sisters all die?
Say it again one more time,
What if everyone I love dies?
They say it's irrational when I think it.
But were you there when she found out
Her father suddenly died?
Were you there when his parents put on a brave
face at a funeral for a 3 year old?
What if my mother dies. Everyone dies,
I can't take this right now,
Am I selfish for wanting to go first?
Lay in bed with me every night,
Let your brain wander; say it one more time.
What if my mom dies tonight?

Poetic Processing

I keep telling myself to write.
It helps me process emotions,
I have already pushed them aside I
Can't find them anymore,
Just snippets of what happened flashing over my
eyes.
Hugging the smallest child as she cries and screams
for her mommy.
My hand on my sister's shoulder
The sound of my fathers booming voice and feeling
myself jump again
My mother pulling me aside and sobbing that she will
leave him
Phone Call from my brother; i never get phone calls
from my brother
What I thought was my sister's lifeless body in the
closet of the bathroom in the back bedroom of the air
bnb that we booked to spread my grandpa jr's ashes.
The tears down my nieces faces
The narrowed eyes and soundless ears during a panic
attack as I scream "where's the meds! How much did
she take?"
My brother in law on the phone with the ambulance
The children crying in the car
Sneaking in snacks from the chaotic house for the
little ones.
My sister's body on the ground.

The looks on my niece's faces.

The sight of the girl I have only known for 3 months
making friendship bracelets with my two oldests
nieces after she had just met my family for the first
time.
Her pulling me aside and reassuring me that she
would never talk to me that way.
Telling her I love her.
Loving her.
Actually truly loving someone who wasn't family, or
my best friends.
The sight of her snuggling my baby nephew
Her holding my sobbing body.
Smoking weed in "the bunkhouse" with my cousins
Stealing them beers
Playing games with my aunt and uncle
Saying "I love you"
Hearing "I love you too"

I am the happiest, and most lost and traumatized that
I have ever been.
How do you process that in a poetic way?

Negligence

drown me in
fire.
i want to feel
the burning feeling
of the air
escaping my lungs.
push me
into
the dirt
no coffin
let the bugs
eat my body
let the grass
cover my grave
no evidence
there was ever
a survivor there

survivor.

unfortunately,
that's who i am
survivor of nothing
worth telling
only a handful of pills

i couldn't get myself to swallow
survivor of
the window
i was too scared to jump from
survivor of
hands wrapped around my throat
far too weak to choke.
survivor of nothing
but negligence
of my own

self-worth.

Sometimes Constantly Maybe

sometimes when you're sick
you're tired
and sometimes
when you're tired
you're sick
 and sometimes
when you're sick
it's because you're depressed
and sometimes
when you're depressed
you're tired
and sometimes
when you're tired
you're depressed
and sometimes
when you're tired
you're just tired
and i feel too
many feelings and
i think too many thoughts
and sometimes
it's the adhd
and sometimes
its the anxiety
and sometimes,
most of the time
its depression and
its always because i am tired

and when i'm not tired
my skin crawls
and when my skin crawls
my hand moves
and when my hand moves
i'm excited
and when i'm excited
i fill with joy
and when it leaves my body
i realize
joy is exhausting
and i'm constantly crying
and constantly smiling
and always so so tired
and possibly depressed
or maybe its my lungs
or maybe it's in my head
it would be if its depression
or maybe, or maybe.
the high kicks in and everything blurs together
suddenly i've written a poem.

Late Night Drives

on our best days and our worst days,
the front doors of our houses carefully shut,
as we sneak out late into the night,
and climb into your 2010 manual car.
windows cranked down, with
cold wind spilling in sending chills
down our backs. the back roads lead the car
up and down the spiraling hills.
the fog always made me nervous,
inhibiting the sight far in front of us.
until we stuck our hands out the window,
feeling the droplets
crawl through our hands, the dangerous
layer of blindness is nothing but bits of water.
the music is particularly picked by our moods,
which is always in tune with each other,
just as your voice is with the sound of
the smiths or florence and the machine,
or penatonix when you taught me how to
enjoy christmas music again
after years of burying friends in december.
every time we get into your car,
the adrenaline of sneaking out with a best friend
drips through my veins, and we feel alive again.
i show you how to let go and cry,
into the darkness
you show me how to let go and scream,
into the abyss.

Patchwork

They tell you every day where each part of your
patchwork "old" soul
Comes from and every day you grieve the piece
of you
That died before you were born,
The one that died when you were 20
They say you look like them, you talk like them
you act like them
But you don't even know who you are
Because every piece of you died before you
really got to shake their hand
And say hello to it. I think I am writing this
because of Dennis
I think I am kindly they say that's from Mary
I want to know how to not lose hope and how to
not fear passion
I ache for what I never got; the memories lost to
being a youngest child
You're just like your siblings, your just like your
mother, your father,
Your aunts, uncles, cousins, grandparents, and
everyone who existed before you,
Because you are not you, you are only what we
can make of you

By patching together the pieces of your identity
with the slightest sliver
Of evidence that you are not you, you are
everyone around you.
And now that they are gone, a piece of you has
died away,
But I will not stop being kind, I will not stop
writing,
For maybe my soul will be patched together by
not the people who came before me
But the people I lived before they even existed.

The Trees and Me

I liked to lay down in the back seat
To watch all the tree branches swing by
As we drive to Oklahoma to see him.
That's the thing about trees in the winter,
Some say they look sad and dead,
But there is no sadness for the
Trees that die every winter,
Because unlike you, the trees will
come back to life in the springtime.
It was cold now and I had no jacket
And had this morning existed when I was a kid
My dad would have yelled
at me that I was going to get sick and die
And looking back I know it was out of love
But as a kid I didn't pick up on those kinds of things.
My brain works differently than most
And you could argue two things
That no body's brain works the same
Or that my brain works just fine
And although both are true my
brain doesn't work like the average one
It has so many bumps in the road
Like the anxiety or the depression or the
adhd or even the grief god the grief
These things shape your brain they change them,
At least I think they do
I never do any research on my own
It's hard for me to read

My therapist says that's why I like poetry
It works for a brain like mine
Fragmented statements that have deeper meaning
I love thinking I love learning
No I don't come to class but I try
I really do, but I was visiting her and
There was a display in the hospital
For how to deal, with all types of grief.
Sudden death,
Death of a spouse,
            Death of a child.
But never for the death of yourself.
Never does it tell you how to deal with
The reality of watching yourself wither away.
Watching the old you slip into just that,
The old you because when the trees
Come back to life in the spring
I'm not sure who will rise again with them.